I0814241

SPY GUIDE

SPY SOCIAL SKILLS

ELSIE OLSON

Abdo & Daughters
MIDDLE GRADE NONFICTION

An imprint of Abdo Publishing
abdobooks.com

ABDOBOOKS.COM

Published by Abdo Publishing, a division of ABDO, PO Box 398166, Minneapolis, Minnesota 55439.

Printed in the United States of America, North Mankato, Minnesota
052024
092024

Design: Kelly Doudna, Mighty Media, Inc.
Production: Mighty Media, Inc.
Editor: Katherine Chu
Cover Photographs: Central Intelligence Agency, Flickr, Library of Congress, Shutterstock Images, Wikimedia Commons

Interior Photographs: Adobe Stock, pp. 19, 23, 59; Alamy Photo, pp. 34, 46; AP Images, pp. 20, 44–45, 52–53, 61 (top left); Central Intelligence Agency, p. 22 (top); Flickr, p. 13; Library of Congress, pp. 29, 32, 33, 35, 60 (bottom left); Shutterstock Images, pp. 1, 4–5, 10–11, 14, 15, 16–17, 18, 30–31, 41, 56, 58–59, 60 (top left), 61 (top right); Wikimedia Commons, pp. 6–7, 8, 22 (bottom), 24–25, 26, 28, 36–37, 38, 40, 42, 43, 48, 49, 50, 55, 60 (top right, bottom middle, bottom right), 61 (bottom left, bottom right)

Design Elements: Adobe Stock

Library of Congress Control Number: 2023949222

Publisher's Cataloging-in-Publication Data
Names: Olson, Elsie, author.
Title: Spy social skills / by Elsie Olson
Description: Minneapolis, Minnesota : Abdo Publishing, 2025 | Series: Spy guide | Includes online resources and index.
Identifiers: ISBN 9781098293161 (lib. bdg.) | ISBN 9798384912439 (ebook)
Subjects: LCSH: Persuasion (Psychology)--Juvenile literature. | Self-defense--Juvenile literature. | Life skills--Juvenile literature. | Espionage--Juvenile literature. | Spies--Juvenile literature.
Classification: DDC 327.12--dc23

CONTENTS

Josephine Baker went through the German checkpoint at Canfranc station when traveling from France to Spain.

CHAPTER 1

HIDDEN IN THE SPOTLIGHT

A GLAMOROUS WOMAN IN A LUXURIOUS FUR COAT stares out the window at the rugged Pyrenees Mountains in France. Her train speeds towards the Spanish border. A mustached man in glasses sits beside her. He seems to be traveling with her to help with her luggage.

It's November 1940, and World War II has been raging for almost a year. For the last six months, France has been under German control. This has taken a great toll on France and many French people are suffering.

The border between France and Spain is closely guarded. Anyone crossing is questioned and searched. Suspected French Resistance fighters are arrested, or worse. But the woman on the train doesn't seem concerned. That's because she isn't just anyone. She is beloved American singer, dancer, and actress Josephine Baker.

THE ROAD TO PORTUGAL

At the border crossing between France and Spain, all eyes are on Baker as she gets off the train, but nobody searches her. Instead, German guards and plainclothes officers are starstruck. They stare as she flashes her famous smile. They ask for her autograph and take her picture.

Baker fascinates the German officers and guards so much, they pay no attention to the man carrying her luggage. But this man happens to be French intelligence agent and Resistance fighter Jacques Abtey in disguise. And Baker's luggage is full of secret information. Her sheet music contains intelligence about German troop movements written in invisible ink. And photographs showing German invasion equipment are safely tucked under Baker's dress.

Abtey and Baker continue traveling to Lisbon, Portugal, a country that remained neutral in the war. Once in Lisbon, Abtey and Baker pass their intelligence to agents at the British embassy. They have completed this mission, but Baker's work is far from over. She will continue to spy on behalf of the French Resistance until the war ends in 1945.

AN UNLIKELY SPY

Baker's road to spydom was surprising to many. She was born in Saint Louis, Missouri, in 1906 and spent

When the war was over, the French Committee of National Liberation awarded Baker the Resistance Medal.

After World War II, Baker continued to perform around the world.

her childhood in extreme poverty. She began singing and dancing as a teenager. She was successful, but as a Black woman, she faced discrimination and racism. At age 19, Baker moved to Paris, France, where she continued to perform. She felt welcome there, so she made Paris her home.

In 1939, Daniel Marouani, Baker's manager and a British informer, introduced Baker to Abtey, suggesting that she be recruited to spy for France. At first, Abtey didn't believe Baker could be an effective spy. Most spies collect their intelligence by hiding in the shadows, and the legendary and glamorous Baker was constantly in the spotlight. But Baker had connections to many powerful people with access to information. And her fame would help protect her from detection. "Oh, nobody would think I'm a spy," she told Abtey when he expressed his concern.

Baker's intuition proved to be correct. After being recruited by Abtey, she charmed almost anyone she met into sharing their secrets. Baker started by gathering information at parties with diplomats from Italy and Japan, which were allied with Germany. She wrote what she learned on her arms and palms.

Later, she toured throughout Europe and North Africa. Everywhere she went, invitations to parties followed. Many party guests were German and Italian officers. Baker used her charm to gather whatever information she could from them. Then, in her hotel room, she jotted what she overheard on notes that she smuggled out in her underwear. Despite the danger of her work and the risks she took, Baker was never caught. As she once said, "Who would dare search Josephine Baker?"

Many spies receive little to no training and must use their own wits to avoid detection.

CHAPTER 2

BECOMING A SPY

JOSEPHINE BAKER'S FAME MADE HER AN UNUSUAL candidate for espionage. Most spies do their best to avoid attention and blend into their surroundings. And at the time, Baker was the most photographed woman in the world. But the fact that she was such an unlikely spy ultimately made her a perfect one. No one suspected her.

THE BIRTH OF A SPY

Espionage is the art of stealing secret information on behalf of a government, intelligence, or military agency. Almost anyone with access to intelligence can become a spy. Some spies are high-ranking government or intelligence officials with access to classified information. But spies do not need to be high-ranking officials. A babysitter for a high-level officer could be a spy. And a janitor or cafeteria worker in an intelligence agency might secretly be working to gather information.

SPYING FOR LOVE AND MONEY

Espionage is dangerous work. Spies caught in the act can be fined, arrested, or worse. Though there is risk, people agree to enter the world of espionage for many different reasons.

Many spies are motivated by patriotism or love for their country. Other spies choose to spy against their home country if they disagree with the actions of their government. In 2001, US Defense Intelligence Agency (DIA) analyst Ana Montes was arrested after spying on behalf of Cuba for about 16 years. Montes became a spy because she disagreed with US foreign policies in Latin America. But not all spies enter the profession for such noble reasons. Some become spies because of blackmail, ego, or greed.

Money is a common motivator for spies. Aldrich Ames, an American officer for the Central Intelligence Agency (CIA), began spying for the Union of Soviet Socialist Republics (USSR), or Soviet Union, in the 1980s.

PAYING A SPY

A spy's motivations can determine the compensation for their work. Soviet spy Dmitri Polyakov began spying for the US because he disagreed with the Soviet government. Because his main motivation for spying was patriotism, Polyakov only asked for $3,000 per year in the form of hunting and fishing equipment and carpentry tools. US spy Robert Hanssen, on the other hand, was motivated by money. The Soviets paid Hanssen $1.4 million in cash, bank funds, and diamonds in exchange for his espionage.

Ames was paid more than $2 million for giving US secrets to the Soviets, including the identities of Soviet spies working for the US. When asked why he had agreed to spy against his country, Ames said, "Money was the motivation."

Spies can also be motivated by love. Michael Walker was a member of the US Navy who passed naval secrets to the USSR. His father, John A. Walker Jr., was the leader of a famous spy ring. Michael said he started spying in part to please his father.

John A. Walker Jr.'s identification documents. Walker also recruited other spies for the USSR. These included family members and one of his friends.

Intelligence officers may learn a new hobby or pretend to share interests with the person they are looking to recruit to get closer to them.

DESIGNING A SPY

While some spies are volunteers, most spies are recruited by intelligence agencies, as Baker was. Recruiting a spy can be delicate work, especially if the intelligence organization is hoping to infiltrate a highly secure location, such as a weapons manufacturing plant. An intelligence agency officer may spend months or years researching and building a relationship with a potential recruit before asking the person to become a spy.

Once a spy has agreed to work for an intelligence agency, they are assigned a handler. This may be the agent who recruited them or a different agent. The handler's job is to help protect the spy and collect the intelligence they gather. The handler may also assist a spy with developing their cover.

THE CHAIN OF INTELLIGENCE

A piece of intelligence gathered by a spy passes through many different hands.

SPY (AGENT, ASSET)

- Collects intelligence

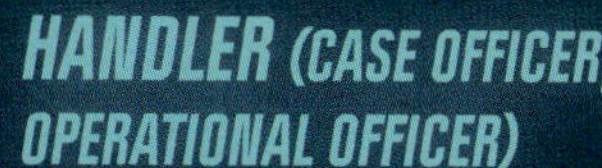

HANDLER (CASE OFFICER, OPERATIONAL OFFICER)

- Recruits and manages the spy
- Plans missions
- Protects the spy's identity
- Collects intelligence from the spy

ANALYST

- Reviews intelligence gathered by spies and other sources
- Determines if the intelligence is reliable
- Consolidates the intelligence into a report

DECISION-MAKER (MILITARY LEADER, LAWMAKER, GOVERNMENT LEADER)

- Reviews the analyst's report
- Decides whether or not to act on the intelligence

A former NOC spy was a business consultant before joining the CIA. Using his previous experience, he posed as a mid-level official to gather information while working for multinational companies.

CHAPTER 3

THE PERFECT COVER

SUCCESSFUL ESPIONAGE REQUIRES A SPY TO PASS COVERT, or secret, information to an intelligence agency without being detected. To do this, spies often work with their handlers to create a cover. This is an identity that allows spies to conceal their espionage activities.

Most spies operate under official cover. This means a spy is posing as an employee of an official government agency, such as a foreign embassy. Spies operating under official cover use their real identities and are protected by their government if caught. But some spies operate under a nonofficial cover (NOC). This is much more challenging and dangerous.

NOC spies infiltrate foreign governments or organizations by pretending to be someone they're not. An NOC spy may pose as a scientist to get a job at a foreign weapons company. Some NOC spies pretend to be businesspeople to work at powerful foreign companies. NOC spies have no official connection with the intelligence agency they work for. This gives them better access to secrets. But it also means they are on their own if they are caught. To stay safe, their covers must be flawless.

CREATING A COVER

The most effective covers use a spy's real identity and are based in reality. For example, a diplomat who works at an embassy or a journalist who regularly meets with people from around the world could become a spy while using their existing job as their cover. Baker's cover as an entertainer was successful because she traveled around the world to perform. So she was able to disguise her espionage activities in her daily routine.

No matter what cover a spy adopts, they must fully commit to it. If a US spy wants a job at a Russian weapons facility, they will need a solid cover to support it. The spy will need to be fluent in the Russian language and culture. They will also need a college degree in physics or engineering with a diploma to prove it. And they will need to create a life story that makes them the perfect candidate

After establishing their cover, a spy may spend years at their job, gaining trust and possibly promotions so they can access secret information or become friends with someone with access.

for the Russian weapons facility job. All these details are part of the legend, or life story, for the spy's cover.

A legend can be a mix of real and false details from the spy's life. It should contain important relationships, such as marriage or children, as well as hobbies and interests. A spy also needs physical evidence to back up any details in the legend. For example, if the legend states the spy has two children in another country, there should be pictures of two children in the spy's home. Or if

WHAT NOT TO DO

Most captured spies are discovered by rival intelligence organizations. Other spies often out them. This is known as getting burned. But spies sometimes blow their cover because they get careless and reveal themselves. One of the most common ways spies blow their cover is by changing their behaviors. A spy can attract attention if they decide to take a late-night walk when they typically go to bed early. Or a spy might suddenly start driving fancy cars or wearing expensive clothes even though they don't make a lot of money.

Spies will also make sure the contents of their pockets match their cover identity. These objects, called pocket litter, make a spy's cover more convincing.

a fishing hobby is part of the spy's cover, they should have fishing equipment in their home and be seen using it.

MASTERS OF DISGUISE

Spies in movies and television shows often sport a variety of wigs, fake noses, mustaches, and elaborate costumes to hide their identities. But modern intelligence agencies can do much more. They can disguise a person's skin color, gender, or facial features with makeup and prosthetics. But more often, spies simply disguise their most obvious features. If a spy has curly hair, they might

JONNA MENDEZ: CHIEF OF DISGUISE

Jonna Mendez became the CIA's chief of disguise in the late 1980s. Her job was to oversee the development of new disguises for the CIA's field agents. In 1991, Mendez met with US president George H.W. Bush while wearing a mask her agency had created. The president was shocked when Mendez pulled off the mask, revealing her true appearance.

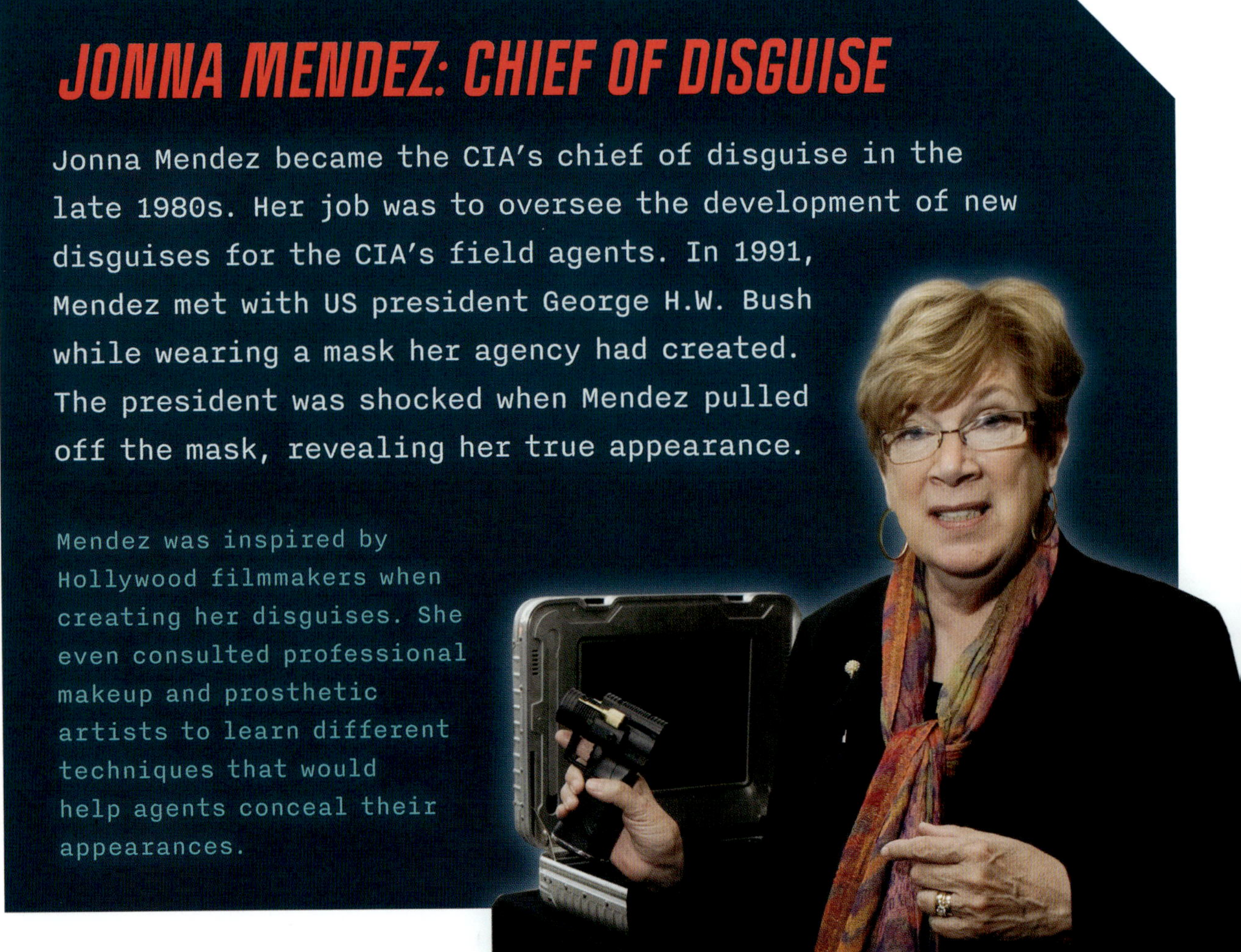

Mendez was inspired by Hollywood filmmakers when creating her disguises. She even consulted professional makeup and prosthetic artists to learn different techniques that would help agents conceal their appearances.

straighten it. A young spy could add streaks of gray to their hair to look older. Glasses and makeup can also quickly change the appearance of a person.

OFFICE OF TECHNICAL SERVICE

The Office of Technical Service (OTS) is a CIA department dedicated to creating modern spy gadgets. Many of these gadgets conceal high-tech espionage devices in everyday objects. A camera might be hidden in a pen. A coat button might contain a secret recording device. And a mobile phone might include lie detection software. To protect its spies, most of the OTS creations are highly classified. Very few people know exactly what the OTS is working on!

Some of the best elements of disguise are the simplest. A spy's clothing should support their cover. Spies might also change the way they walk and talk. Even the way a person stands can suggest what country they are from. A spy who wants to blend in may walk with a slumped posture and wear neutral clothing. A spy who is posing as a powerful diplomat might wear expensive clothing and walk with confidence. To protect their cover, spies must become talented actors who play the same role 24 hours a day, sometimes for years.

TOOLS OF THE TRADE: COVER AND INFILTRATE EDITION

DISGUISE KIT

In the 1970s and 1980s, all CIA operations officers received a disguise kit to help conceal their identities if needed. It included wigs, glasses, mascara, and hair dye.

The Directorate of Science & Technology is a CIA organization that uses technology to collect and protect intelligence. It also works to create gadgets, such as this disguise kit.

LIPSTICK PISTOL

A gun disguised as lipstick was used by female KGB agents during the Cold War. It allowed a female agent to carry a weapon without compromising her cover.

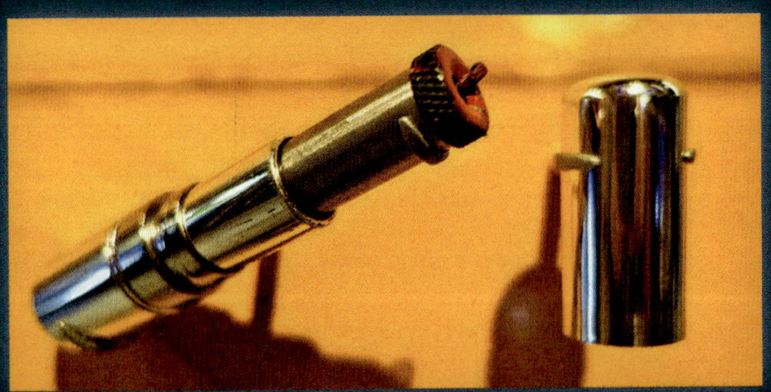

Also known as the "kiss of death," this lipstick pistol was used in the 1960s. The firing mechanism was activated by pressing the barrel into the victim.

FIVE-SECOND FACE MASK

This full-face mask could be applied without a mirror in five seconds or less. It allowed the wearer to instantly transform into someone else, changing their ethnicity, gender, and facial features. Each mask was custom made, so it fit perfectly over the spy's real face. It took ten years to develop the technology, and when or how it was used is still classified.

ANTI-FACIAL RECOGNITION MASK

This mask can fool facial-recognition technology. When the wearer's face is scanned by a camera with facial-recognition tech, their identity comes up as a different person.

GHILLIE SUIT

A ghillie suit is a full-body outfit designed to completely camouflage a person in the surrounding natural environment.

Ghillie suits are mostly worn by special operators and intelligence collectors and help them hide in plain sight.

Multiple plots to free Mary threatened the reign of Elizabeth I (*pictured*), such as the Northern Rebellion of 1569 and the Ridolfi plot.

CHAPTER 4

EARLY ESPIONAGE AND DOUBLE AGENTS

QUEEN ELIZABETH I WAS THE QUEEN OF ENGLAND IN THE LATE 1500s. She was the most powerful woman in the world. But because she was Protestant, her reign was far from secure. The Catholic Church and its supporters felt the crown rightfully belonged to Elizabeth's cousin Mary Stuart, known as Mary, Queen of Scots.

Though Elizabeth imprisoned Mary, many of Elizabeth's subjects still supported her cousin. So Elizabeth was under constant threat of assassination and needed information. She turned to her secretary of state, Sir Francis Walsingham, who started developing a large network of spies. One of his most unexpected and effective spies was Catholic priest Gilbert Gifford, code-named "No. 4."

As a priest, Gifford had access to many people and places Walsingham's other spies didn't. And because he was Catholic, no one suspected him of working for Elizabeth. Gifford even developed a friendship with Mary and smuggled coded letters for her. But he first passed the letters to Walsingham, who had them decoded. Some of the letters contained information on a plan to assassinate Elizabeth. Elizabeth later used these letters as proof to charge and execute Mary for treason.

DOUBLE AGENTS

Although Gifford's intelligence was responsible for Mary's execution, many modern historians believe he was a double agent. This is a spy who pretends to spy for one government or intelligence agency while secretly spying for another. Many believe Gifford started out as a spy for Mary. But after being arrested by Walsingham, Gifford agreed to work for him. Throughout the time Gifford was spying for Walsingham, he was also likely giving intelligence to Mary's supporters, too.

Like Gifford, many spies choose to become double agents when they are caught

Walsingham also sent spies to other countries to gather information on foreign political and military plans.

by the government they are spying on. This is called turning a spy. Some spies can even become triple agents! They work as a spy for one government while pretending to be a double agent for a different government. Gifford was not the first double agent, and he wouldn't be the last. In 1775, England went to war against its American colonies, which were fighting for independence. And double agents were everywhere.

FROM ENSLAVED PERSON TO SPY

James Armistead was one of the most famous double agents during the American Revolution. He was enslaved by a man named William Armistead. Young James spent most of his early life on a plantation in Virginia. In 1781, he agreed to spy for Continental general Marquis de Lafayette.

At the beginning of the war, the British offered freedom to enslaved people who left their American owners to fight for the British. So James Armistead entered British general Lord Charles Cornwallis's headquarters, pretending to be an escaped enslaved person who wanted to spy for the British in exchange for his freedom. To the British, James Armistead seemed like a natural spy. He was familiar with the local area, and since he was an escaped enslaved person, the British never questioned his loyalty. Also, many officers thought enslaved people were less intelligent and not a threat. So, James Armistead could also easily travel between British and American military camps without drawing attention.

The entire time James Armistead claimed to serve the British, he reported back to General Lafayette. James Armistead

« SPY HALL OF FAME »

ANN BATES

James Armistead Lafayette wasn't the only Revolutionary War spy to use his status to conceal his espionage. American schoolteacher Ann Bates used her status as a woman to become a British spy. Bates was the wife of a British soldier and had strong Loyalist sympathies. Because of this, the British recruited her as a spy, paying her a small pension for her help. She disguised herself as a peddler and walked around American military camps, pretending to sell goods. At the time, women were rarely involved in military activities, so Bates wasn't questioned. Once in the camps, she eavesdropped on conversations between soldiers and counted weaponry. She passed this intelligence back to her British handlers. During a mission in one of American general George Washington's camps in 1778, Bates overheard intelligence about a planned invasion of Rhode Island. She then warned the British, who were able to prepare for the attack.

Because she was not seen as a threat, Bates was able to access Washington's headquarters multiple times.

provided intelligence about British troop movements and numbers. Meanwhile, he gave Cornwallis false information about American military strategy.

In September 1781, James Armistead sent General Lafayette his most important message yet. Cornwallis was preparing to move 10,000 British troops to Yorktown, Virginia. Because of that message, the Americans surprised the British with a full blockade. Cornwallis surrendered on October 19, ending the war and securing James Armistead's status as one of the most important double agents in history.

After the war, General Lafayette helped free James Armistead from slavery, so James Armistead took Lafayette as his surname to show his gratitude.

Belle Boyd's activities were infamous by 1862. The press nicknamed her "the Siren of the Shenandoah," "La Belle Rebelle," "the Rebel Joan of Arc," and "Amazon of Secessia."

CHAPTER 5

SPYING AT HOME

IN MAY 1862, A GROUP OF UNION OFFICERS MET IN A HOTEL room in Front Royal, Virginia, to strategize. The Civil War had started a little over a year ago, and Front Royal was serving as the Union's Virginia headquarters. The Union army was larger and better armed than the Confederate army, but that hadn't stopped a string of Confederate victories. The Union army needed to act. So, the officers met and discussed their orders to march east as well as the details of their troop positions and numbers.

If the officers had paid more attention, they might have noticed a teenage girl listening through a small hole in the door. And they might have seen her ride on horseback into the night. She rode 15 miles (24 km) to deliver what she overheard to Confederate officers. Later that month, that same girl rode through a battle just to deliver a message to Confederate general Thomas J. "Stonewall" Jackson. This wasn't just any teenage girl. This was Confederate spy Belle Boyd.

MAKING THE MOST OF MISPERCEPTIONS

During the Civil War, an espionage age blossomed. Because the war was fought entirely on US soil, both sides shared a language, history, and culture. Many Union supporters lived in the South, and many Confederate supporters lived in the North. This meant spies could easily move between armies, disguising their true intentions.

At the time, many people believed that Black people and women were less intelligent than white men. Because of this, military officials didn't expect Black people or women to serve as spies. So many of the most successful spies, like James Armistead Lafayette and Belle Boyd, used these racist and sexist stereotypes to their advantage. They could easily move around and access certain secure areas without drawing suspicion.

With Boyd's help, General Jackson captured the town he was attacking. He wrote a letter to Boyd after the attack, thanking her for her bravery and assistance.

Boyd's aunt was the owner of the hotel where Union officers met. So Boyd was often found socializing in the hotel's lobby. She was charming and popular with the Union soldiers and officers who stayed at the hotel. She was so charming, in fact, that they often let military secrets slip in her presence, never suspecting this intelligence was making its way straight to Jackson. After all, Boyd was just a teenage girl.

ELIZABETH VAN LEW

Elizabeth Van Lew was a wealthy Southerner living in Richmond, Virginia, the Confederate capital. Van Lew appeared to be fully committed to the Confederate cause. But many historians believe she was one of the Union Army's most successful spies.

During the war, Van Lew convinced a Confederate general to let

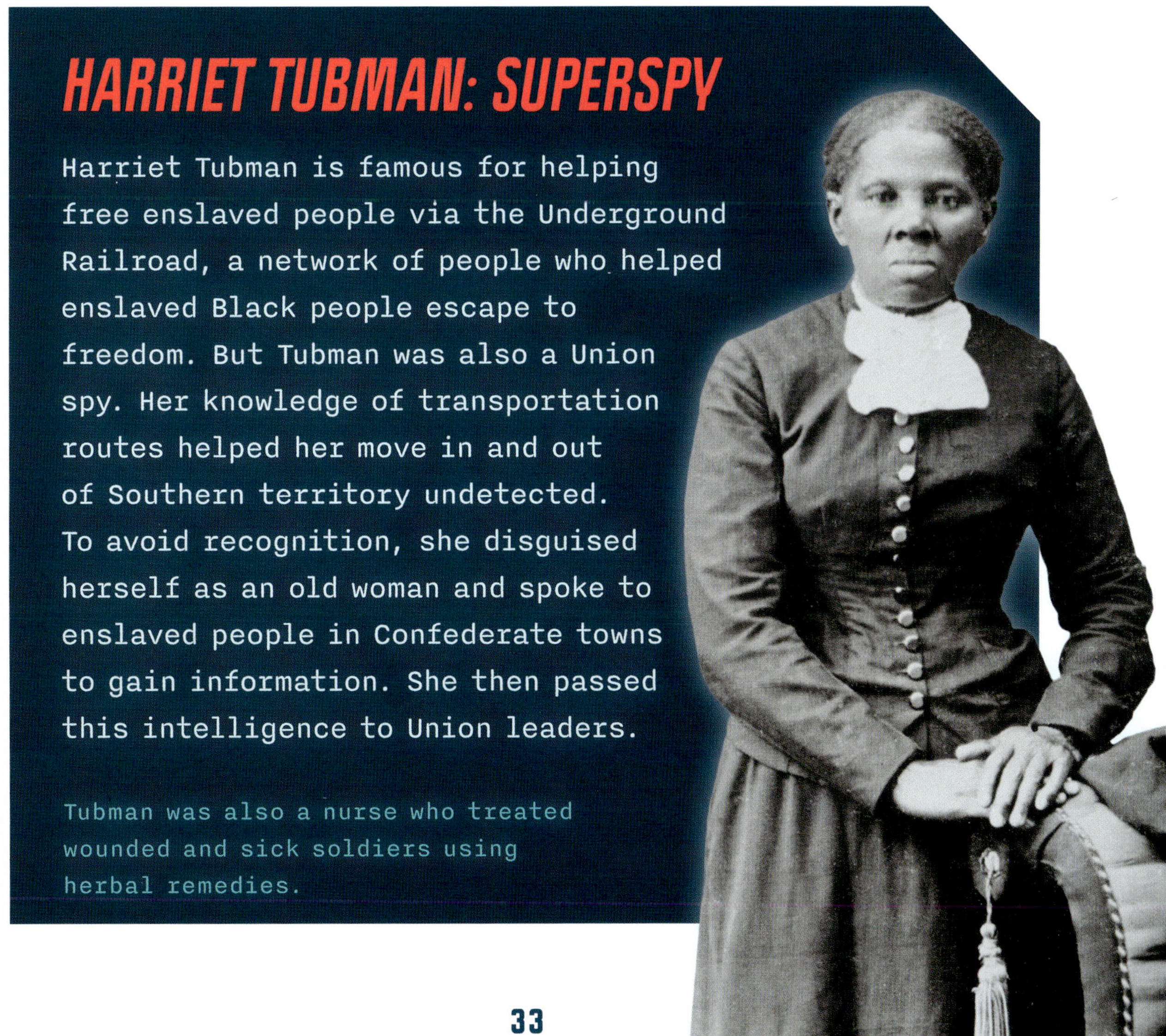

HARRIET TUBMAN: SUPERSPY

Harriet Tubman is famous for helping free enslaved people via the Underground Railroad, a network of people who helped enslaved Black people escape to freedom. But Tubman was also a Union spy. Her knowledge of transportation routes helped her move in and out of Southern territory undetected. To avoid recognition, she disguised herself as an old woman and spoke to enslaved people in Confederate towns to gain information. She then passed this intelligence to Union leaders.

Tubman was also a nurse who treated wounded and sick soldiers using herbal remedies.

her care for Union prisoners as an act of compassion. She began her espionage career by helping the prisoners escape and passing messages to and from the prison. To avoid suspicion, she let the prison warden live at her mansion. Word of Van Lew's skill in passing covert messages and gathering intelligence spread throughout the Union. In 1863, Van Lew became a spymaster for a network of spies based in Richmond.

Van Lew's spy ring contained about a dozen people. It included government officials as well as Black and white citizens who could move freely around Richmond. These agents reported to Van Lew, who sent coded letters to Union leaders written in invisible ink. In 1865, the Confederate Army surrendered and the war ended. Afterward, Union general and future US president Ulysses S. Grant wrote to Van Lew saying, "You have sent me the most valuable information received from Richmond during the war."

Van Lew wrote her thoughts on slavery and the Confederates in a secret diary. She buried it in her backyard and didn't reveal its existence until she was on her deathbed.

« SPY HALL OF FAME »

MARY JANE RICHARDS

One of the most important members of Van Lew's spy ring was her personal servant, Mary Jane Richards. According to Van Lew's diary, "When I open my eyes in the morning, I say to the servant, 'What news, Mary?' and my caterer never fails! Most generally our reliable news is gathered from negroes, and they certainly show wisdom, discretion, and prudence, which is wonderful." In addition to spying for Van Lew, Richards also helped Van Lew care for US Army prisoners in Richmond.

Richards entered Confederate president Jefferson Davis's home (*pictured*) posing as a servant looking for work. She was taken to his office, where she looked at documents in his cabinet.

Mata Hari means "eye of the day" or "sun" in the Malay language.

CHAPTER 6

LOVE AND WAR

MATA HARI SEEMED LIKE THE PERFECT SPY. SHE SPOKE multiple languages and was a dancer who traveled Europe performing for the wealthy. Even with the travel restrictions during World War I, border crossings were never a problem for her. She was famous for her ability to charm rich and powerful men into doing almost anything for her. And Mata Hari had a history of reinventing herself.

Mata Hari was born as Margaretha Zelle in the Netherlands in 1876. She married as a teenager but was abused by her husband, so she left the marriage. With no money or opportunities, she moved to Paris, France, for a fresh start in 1902. There she adopted the name Mata Hari and began performing for small crowds. She told people she was a dancer from India, Malaysia, or Indonesia, depending on who asked. Her exotic style of dancing became a sensation, and soon, she was performing all over Europe.

Mata Hari was blamed for the death of up to 50,000 French soldiers. Though no evidence supported this claim, the court still found her guilty.

THE DANCER SPY

When World War I broke out in 1914, the Netherlands remained a neutral country. As a Dutch citizen, Mata Hari could move freely between countries without suspicion. She also had relationships with many high-ranking politicians and military officials. Because of this, Mata Hari's German connections saw an opportunity. The German secret service recruited Mata Hari and began paying her to spy for them.

In 1915, a French intelligence official asked Mata Hari to spy for the Allies. She agreed, not mentioning that Germany was already paying her to spy for them. Mata Hari was now a double agent.

In 1917, German intelligence officials allowed the French to learn that Mata Hari was their spy. Many historians believe this was because she asked for too much money for her information. A few months later, French officials arrested the dancer and executed her for espionage. Mata Hari's espionage career was short and unsuccessful. But that didn't stop her from becoming one of the most famous spies in history.

LEGACY OR LEGEND?

Espionage is built on secrecy, which means some of the best spy stories are never told. Modern historians believe many famous spies, including Mata Hari and Belle Boyd, probably didn't provide much meaningful intelligence to their handlers. But that didn't stop these women and other spies from becoming infamous in the history of spydom.

SEDUCING SECRETS

Mata Hari wasn't the first or last spy to use romance to gather secrets. Throughout history, spies have traded love for intelligence. This usually involved female spies stealing secrets from male government or military officials. But as World War II ended in the mid-1940s, men also used this technique with great success.

At the end of World War II, Germany was divided into East Germany and West Germany. East Germany was allied with the USSR, and West Germany was allied with Europe and the US. This caused great distrust between the two sides.

Amy Elizabeth Thorpe, also known as Betty Pack, helped the Allies during World War II by romancing men to gain access to secret information.

Millions of young German men died in World War II. So, after the war, many West German women took jobs in military, government, and intelligence services. However, the lack of men eligible for work also meant fewer

HONEY TRAPS

Many intelligence agencies have been known to use a method called a honey trap to gain information. In a honey trap, an agent works to develop a romantic relationship with a target who has access to secret information. The agent can then observe the target, steal information, and convince the target to share secrets.

Sometimes, an agent will use a honey trap to turn their target into a willing spy.

RAVENS AND SWALLOWS

Throughout the Cold War, the USSR also relied on romance to gather intelligence. The KGB, a Soviet intelligence agency, trained men and women for this purpose. Male spies were known as Ravens, and female spies were known as Swallows. These spies targeted foreigners, particularly US soldiers stationed in the USSR. First the spy developed a romantic relationship with their target. Then, they would gather intelligence and often blackmail their target into spying for the USSR.

US propaganda posters were used to warn people to watch out for spies. But they also scared people into thinking spies were everywhere.

men for the young women to date and marry. East Germany saw this as an opportunity.

ROMEOS AND JULIETS

East German intelligence officer Markus Wolf recruited and trained a group of young men, code-named "Romeos," to charm women, code-named "Juliets." Each Juliet held a job with access to intelligence. Wolf trained the Romeos in the art of espionage, gave them false identities, and sent them to West Germany to find a woman to target. Romeos researched their targets to learn their backgrounds, likes, and dislikes. Then they would start a romantic relationship to gain access to their Juliet's secrets.

Western intelligence named Markus Wolf "the man without a face" because they didn't know what he looked like. He was finally identified by East German defector Werner Stiller in 1979.

Russia awarded Norwood the Order of the Red Banner for her work. The KGB also described her as "a committed, reliable, and disciplined agent."

CHAPTER 7

COLD WAR COVER

ON A CRISP SEPTEMBER DAY IN 1999, SURPRISED NEIGHBORS and eager reporters swarmed the London home of 87-year-old Melita Norwood. Norwood's neighbors knew her as a sweet old lady who baked pies, made delicious jams, and carefully nurtured a rose garden. The people closest to her never would have guessed the secret Norwood was about to share with reporters.

When Norwood stepped out of her house, she confirmed something her own daughter didn't even know. She was a Soviet spy. For nearly 40 years, she had spied on the British, making her the Soviet's longest-serving spy.

In 1932, the British Non-Ferrous Metals Research Association hired young Norwood as a secretary. The company was secretly developing nuclear technology. In 1943, Norwood started working for department head G.L. Bailey. Bailey was high up in the company, which meant he had access to all the company's nuclear secrets. And so did Norwood.

Norwood refused to take any money from her KGB handlers, believing it could be traced back to her.

AN UNLIKELY SPY

Norwood was a proud Communist. She believed that the USSR's government would help the Soviets. During the Cold War, the US, with the help of Great Britain, was competing with the Soviets to develop weapons. Norwood was worried that if the US and Great Britain succeeded in the weapons race, Soviet people would suffer.

When a KGB agent recruited Norwood and asked her to share British nuclear secrets with the Soviets, she agreed. KGB agents code-named Norwood "Hola." When she was alone, Norwood snuck into Bailey's safe, photographed documents, then put them back. She met with Soviet handlers near her suburban London home to pass off the photos. If she was late getting home, she told her husband it was due to traffic.

Norwood retired from her job and espionage career in 1972.

But her espionage wasn't discovered until the 1990s, when a captured KGB officer revealed the identities of several agents. Norwood's cover held for so long because her life seemed so ordinary. Even when British intelligence agents knew there was a mole in their nuclear program, they didn't suspect Norwood. Most agents at the time didn't believe a woman was capable of such effective spying, especially a woman as seemingly unremarkable as Norwood.

THE KGB

During the Cold War, the KGB was the intelligence organization for the USSR's Communist Party. It was charged with gathering foreign intelligence, often through espionage. But the group also acted as a secret police force during the Cold War. The KGB ended with the collapse of the USSR in 1991.

SPY VS. SPY

The intelligence industry thrived during the Cold War, with hundreds of thousands of spies like Norwood working to gather state secrets. Countries around the world established and grew huge intelligence agencies to manage their espionage activity. The USSR had the KGB and GRU. Britain had MI5 and MI6. And the US had the US Federal Bureau of Investigation (FBI) and the CIA.

During the Cold War, the US and its allies, including Britain and France, were rivals with the USSR and its allies. These countries never openly fought one another during this time. Instead, the

Klaus Fuchs was a Soviet spy who worked as a scientist for the US-led Manhattan Project, which created nuclear weapons. Like Norwood, he also passed secret information to the Soviets.

nations waged secret battles using information to keep their rivals from gaining too much power. Spies were their eyes and ears on the ground, and they were everywhere. People on both sides of the conflict found themselves suspecting their friends, neighbors, and coworkers of secretly spying for their enemy.

FBI AND CIA

The two best-known US intelligence agencies are the FBI and the CIA. The FBI was founded in 1908 to combat crime. It gathers intelligence from US citizens and enforces US laws. The CIA was founded in 1947 to gather foreign intelligence. It is not allowed to gather intelligence from US citizens and cannot act on any information it receives. Instead, CIA officials must share the information with government leaders or law enforcement agencies, who decide how to respond to the information.

Many historians believe the intelligence provided by spies during the Cold War helped keep the tension from exploding into open war. Spies reported on political leaders, their decisions, and the enemy's strategies. They also often spread false information,

US courts convicted Soviet spies Julius and Ethel Rosenberg of espionage in 1951 and sentenced them to death. As of 2023, they were the only US civilians executed for espionage.

« SPY HALL OF FAME »

JOHN MULHOLLAND

In the 1950s, during the peak of the Cold War, the CIA hired professional magician John Mulholland to write a manual for its spies. Magicians are famous for using misdirection, diversion, and psychological illusions to fool their audiences. CIA officials believed these same tactics could help spies avoid detection. Mulholland's manual is titled *The Official CIA Manual of Trickery and Deception*. It includes tips for how to secretly take an object from someone and how to use a shoelace pattern to pass a message. But some of Mulholland's most useful tips are techniques to help a spy appear stupid and nonthreatening. According to Mulholland, acting like a fool is one of the most powerful forms of misdirection. The manual was part of a larger CIA project known as MK-ULTRA. The project's mission was to develop and perfect mind-control techniques that could be used against Soviet enemies.

The CIA paid Mulholland $3,000 to write the manual. Although many thought it was destroyed in 1973, a copy was found by two intelligence agents who published it in 2009.

known as misinformation, misleading their enemy. Double agents reported directly on the activities of rival intelligence organizations and even sabotaged their work. And spies hidden in weapons and technology manufacturing companies, like Norwood, provided technical information that kept one country from gaining a major technological advantage over another.

BECOMING AN AGENT

Getting a job at the CIA or FBI is a sure way to find yourself on the front lines of covert intelligence. To become a CIA or FBI agent, you must be a US citizen with a college degree. It also helps to speak more than one language. Aspiring agents need to pass a background check and complete a lengthy application process. They also need to pass medical and fitness requirements before beginning a rigorous training program.

The FBI and CIA were watching the Guryev family for years and had bugged and secretly searched their house when they weren't home.

CHAPTER 8

MODERN SPYING AND DEEP COVER

TO THEIR NEIGHBORS, THE MURPHYS SEEMED LIKE A perfectly ordinary American family. They lived in a two-story home on a quiet street in Montclair, New Jersey. Cynthia was a financial planner who worked in nearby New York City. Richard was a stay-at-home dad who cared for the couple's two young daughters, Kate and Lisa.

The family wasn't overly social, but they showed up at neighborhood block parties. Cynthia frequently walked the family dog through the neighborhood. And one summer, Kate and Lisa even ran a lemonade stand.

In 2010, the Murphys' seemingly all-American image was shattered when FBI agents raided their home, revealing the Murphys' true identities. Cynthia and Richard Murphy were really Lidiya and Vladimir Guryev. And they were Russian spies.

DEEP COVER

The Guryevs were part of an infamous spy ring investigated by the FBI's Operation Ghost Stories. Their mission was to steal US political secrets and if possible, even influence US politics. Although they were ultimately unsuccessful, the Russian spies' ruse became one of the most well-known deep-cover operations in US history. Deep-cover operations are long-term espionage missions in which spies spend years or decades working to build a cover to gain access to intelligence.

The Guryevs had been undercover since the mid-1990s. The couple came to the US so Lidiya could study at Columbia University. Her mission at the time was to provide details about the school's faculty to her Russian handlers. Eventually, Lidiya got a job in finance, giving her access to global financial information. She worked to form friendships with people who had political connections, all the while reporting back to her handlers.

For 20 years, the Guryevs remained in deep cover, living under their fake identities. Vladimir claimed to have been born in Pennsylvania and Lidiya in New York City. Their daughters were born and raised in America. The Guryevs tried to blend into US society and even refused to speak Russian in their home. The FBI surveilled and gathered intelligence on the members of the spy ring for years. Once they found and identified all the members, the FBI arrested them. Shortly after their arrest, the Guryevs and their daughters were sent to Russia as part of a prisoner exchange.

Richard Murphy (Vladimir Guryev)

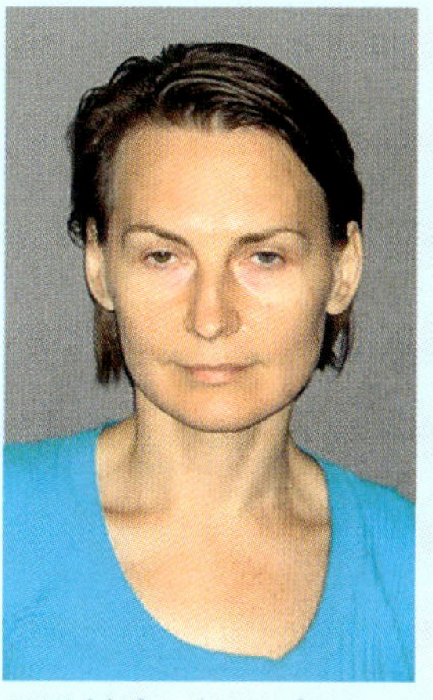

Cynthia Murphy (Lidiya Guryev)

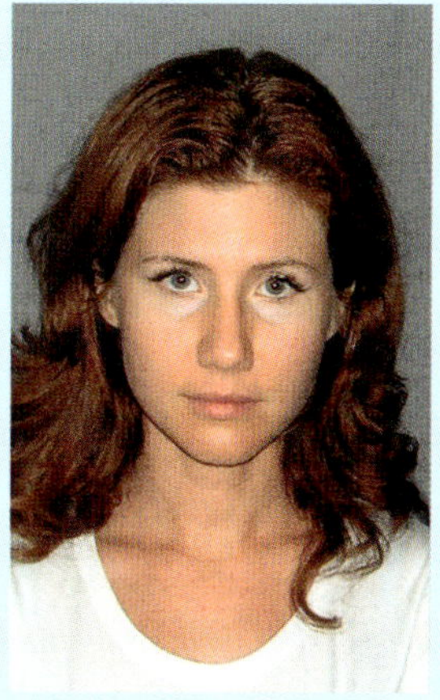

Anna Chapman (Anna Kushchenko)

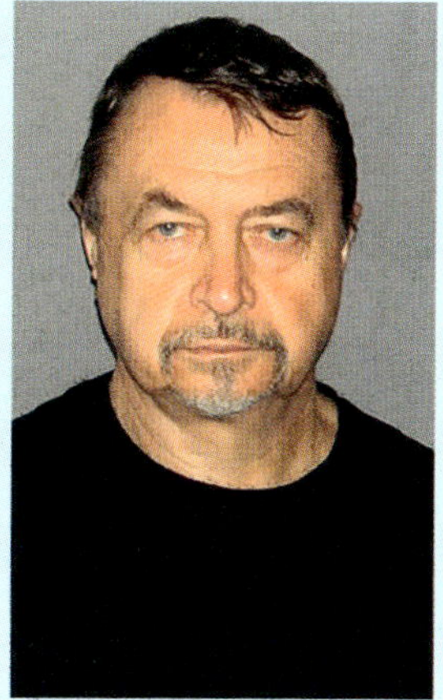

Juan Lazaro (Mikhail Vasenkov)

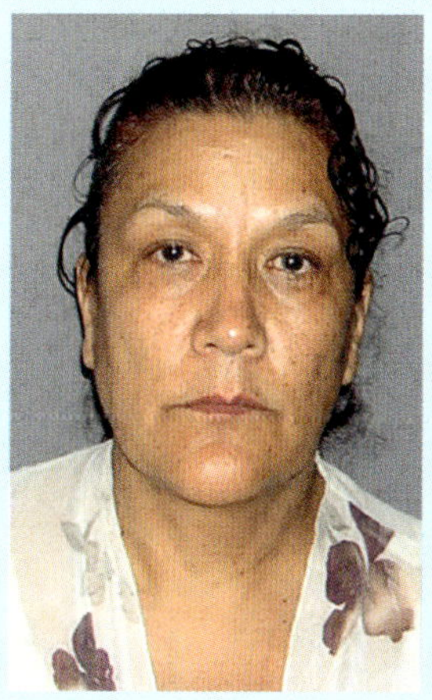

Vicky Peláez

Donald Heathfield (Andrey Bezrukov)

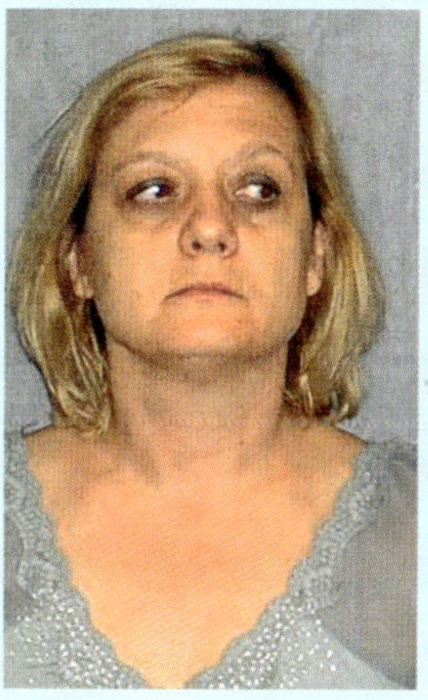

Tracey Foley (Elena Vavilova)

Michael Zottoli (Mikhail Kutsik)

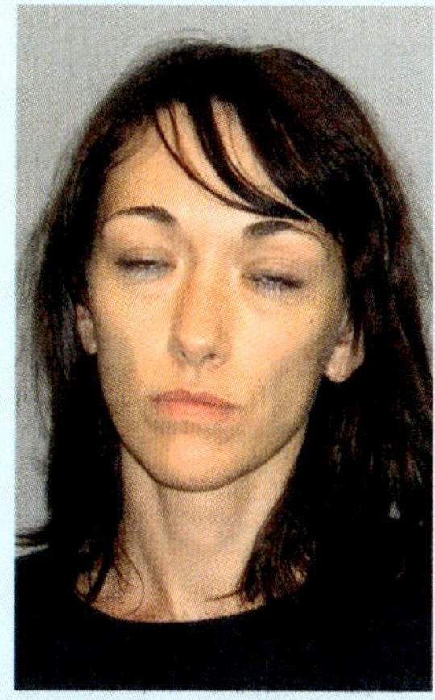

Patricia Mills (Nataliya Pereverzeva)

Mikhail Semenko

Operation Ghost Stories investigated ten highly trained Russian spies who engaged in long-term espionage activities under false identities.

SLEEPER AGENTS

Deep-cover spies are often sleeper agents. These are spies who infiltrate a foreign country or intelligence agency. The agent becomes inactive and may live an ordinary life, establishing their cover for months, years, or maybe forever. Eventually, many of these spies are activated, or called into action. The agent then begins undertaking espionage activities.

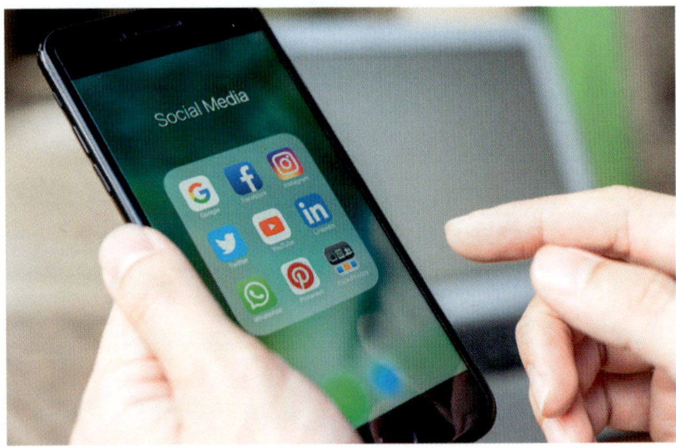

Modern spies try to access intelligence by using social media sites. From 2021 to 2022, UK intelligence agency MI5 found over 10,000 "disguised approaches" targeting the UK's national security.

A NEW AGE OF ESPIONAGE

Modern espionage activities rely more on technology, such as drones and satellites, than secret agents. But spies still work to infiltrate governments, terrorist organizations, and crime rings around the world. And not all modern spies work for official intelligence agencies. Many work for private companies, especially tech and finance companies. Some corporations even hire individuals to spy on their behalf. Corporate spies work to steal secret information from a company's competitor.

No matter who they are spying on, the rise of social media makes posing as a different person easier than ever. Modern spies can develop a fake social media profile in a matter of minutes.

They can also use these false identities to connect and build relationships with targets thousands of miles away. In 2019, Pakistani spies set up fake social media profiles to target Indian soldiers. The operation worked so well that India asked its soldiers to remove their social media accounts from their phones and computers.

Spying is often a lonely and dangerous profession. Spies who are caught face serious consequences. And the spies who avoid detection often disappear into history. The best spies may receive little or no credit for the risks they take. Still, many people are drawn to espionage because it is exciting, challenging, and makes a difference. The art of espionage can help make the world a safer place.

DEEP COVER IN THE INTERNET AGE

The rise of the internet and social media makes it easy to establish a short-term cover. But it makes building a long-term cover much more challenging. An agent can easily set up a social media account using a false identity. They can even create fake online records showing when they graduated school, bought a house, or started a job. However, all internet records are dated. This means an intelligence official who analyzes the digital records can learn when each one was created. If the records were all made in the same day or year, the official knows they likely have a spy on their hands.

SO YOU WANT TO BE A SPY?

Spies can be anywhere and everywhere. Your mom's boss, your next-door neighbor, or even your teacher could be a spy! Almost anyone can become a spy. But being a spy who can infiltrate an organization isn't easy. Do you have what it takes to create a cover? Complete the missions below to find out!

MISSION 1
CREATE A LEGEND

WHAT YOU NEED

pencil

paper

Start creating a legend for a false identity using details that support your cover. Include information about your family, friends, early life, likes, dislikes, hobbies, and more. Remember, the best legends blend true and false details to create a convincing story. Test your legend by telling it to a friend. See if they can guess which details are true and which are false.

MISSION 2
DESIGN YOUR DISGUISE

WHAT YOU NEED

mirror costume supplies

Now that your legend is ready, it's time to create your disguise. Look in the mirror and carefully pay attention to the physical features people are most likely to notice about you, such as the color of your hair or your glasses. How can you temporarily alter these features? Try changing your clothes, wearing a wig, putting on a hat, or wearing sunglasses. Experiment with changing your features until you have the perfect disguise.

MISSION 3
MASTER YOUR MEMORY

WHAT YOU NEED

timer pencil paper art supplies

You've probably seen all kinds of cool spy gadgets in movies and on television. But a spy's greatest tool is their brain. Study the image to the left closely for one minute. Try to notice as many details as possible. When the time is up, close the book. Write down as many details as you can possibly remember. Use these details to recreate the photograph. Compare your drawing to the original photo. How accurate is your memory?

TIMELINE

Sir Francis Walsingham operates a spy network on behalf of Queen Elizabeth I. One of his spies is likely double agent, Catholic priest Gilbert Gifford.
LATE 1500s

The American Revolutionary War
1775–1783

Belle Boyd spies for the Confederate Army.
1862

World War I
1914–1918

Mata Hari is executed for espionage for spying against the French.
1917

1861–1865
The American Civil War

1781
James Armistead agrees to spy for Continental general Marquis de Lafayette.

1863
Elizabeth Van Lew becomes spymaster of a network of Union spies based in Richmond, Virginia.

1939
French intelligence agent Jacques Abtey recruits Josephine Baker as a spy.

1939–1945
World War II

East Germany begins its Romeo and Juliet program, training a group of young men to charm West German women with access to intelligence.
LATE 1940s

The Cold War
1947–1991

Former British secretary Melita Norwood reveals she spied for the USSR for almost 40 years.
1999

Pakistani spies set up fake social media profiles to target Indian soldiers.
2019

1953
Magician John Mulholland writes *The Official CIA Manual of Trickery and Deception* to help train CIA spies.

2001
DIA analyst Ana Montes is arrested after spying on behalf of Cuba for almost 16 years.

2010
The FBI raids the home of Russian deep-cover agents Lidiya and Vladimir Guryev, known as Cynthia and Richard Murphy.

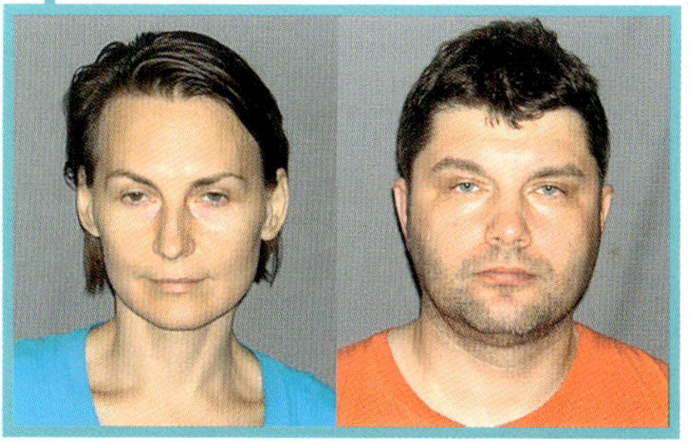

GLOSSARY

analyst—a person who determines the meaning of something by breaking down its parts.

assassination—the murder of a very important person, usually for political reasons.

blockade—the cutting off of an area by soldiers or ships. A blockade prevents supplies and people from going into or out of an area.

Civil War—the war between the United States of America and the Confederate States of America from 1861 to 1865.

classified—kept from the public in order to protect national security.

diversion—something that draws the attention of an enemy away.

eavesdrop—to secretly listen to a private conversation.

espionage—the secret gathering of information on others.

ethnicity—the relation to a group of people based on a common race, nationality, religion, or culture.

exotic—different or unusual.

facial recognition—a way of identifying or confirming an individual's identity using their face.

gender—the behaviors, characteristics, and qualities most often associated with either the male or female sex.

infiltrate—to enter a place secretly and without permission.

intuition—the power of knowing immediately and without conscious reasoning.

misdirection—making people pay attention to the wrong thing so they will not notice something else.

mole—a spy who establishes a long-term cover within an organization.

potential—having the ability to occur or be achieved in the future.

prosthetic—of, relating to, or being an artificial device that replaces a part of the body.

sabotage—to harm an enemy nation's defenses by damaging or destroying something on purpose.

sexist—related to the unfair treatment of people because of their sex.

state secret—a piece of information kept secret by the government.

strategize—to lay out careful plans.

ONLINE RESOURCES

To learn more about spy social skills, please visit **abdobooklinks.com** or scan this QR code. These links are routinely monitored and updated to provide the most current information available.

INDEX